CLOSING A SALE

Ten tips to turn prospects into customers

Written by Irène Guittin
Translated by Rebecca Neal

CLOSING A SALE

- **Problem:** what tools and techniques can you use to turn prospects into customers?
- **Uses:** knowing how to set out your arguments and behave around potential clients will enable you to boost your sales figures and generate customer loyalty.
- **Professional context:** sales optimisation, customer relationships, business.
- **FAQs:**
  - How long should a sale take?
  - The customer has their heart set on a particular product, but I do not think it is right for them. What should I do?
  - Should I provide an exhaustive description of the product's features?
  - Is it better to conceal the product's weak points or to be transparent?
  - A customer is taking up a lot of my time while I have others waiting for me. How can I cut the conversation short without losing them?
  - The customer seems to be won over, but

they want to make the purchase later. How can I close the sale now?
  - The customer wants to compare my offer with the competition. How can I get them to buy from me?
  - What should I say to the customer to win their loyalty?

Sales can be very rewarding, in that sellers help the customer to solve a particular problem and ideally leave them satisfied. They also have the opportunity to showcase their knowledge of the product, their decision-making skills and their powers of persuasion.

Nonetheless, sales can prove frustrating, as there are a number of pitfalls to avoid and sellers need to constantly work to improve their performance. This means that it is essential to understand how the exchange with the customer works, in order to optimise your relationship with them. In his celebrated treatise *The Art of War*, the Chinese general Sun Tzu (6th-5th centuries BC) wrote: "We cannot enter into alliances until we are acquainted with the designs of our neighbours". The same principle applies to sales, which means that if you want to reach an agreement with a potential customer, you must know what their objectives are.

Furthermore, all communication, including – and perhaps especially – business communication is based on trust between the two parties. All sales techniques therefore aim to reassure the customer and encourage them to trust both the seller and the product.

While selling does not come naturally to everyone, there are a few easy, straightforward techniques that you can use to boost your sales performance. In 50 minutes, you will discover ten tried-and-tested tips to close a sale and set you on your way to becoming the next Joe Girard (world-record-breaking car salesman, born in 1928).

EFFECTIVE SALES: THE BASICS

For customers, there is nothing worse than feeling ignored by the sales assistants in a shop. To ensure that your potential customers do not feel abandoned, you need to show them that you are there to help as soon as they arrive.

1. Greet the customer

Sellers should always be the ones to open a dialogue. Continuing with what you are doing without paying attention to the prospect and waiting for them to come to you is an all-too-common mistake. It is up to you to approach the customer.

Of course, you must be smiling when you approach the customer. However, if the customer sees that your smile is forced or insincere, it will have a negative effect; instead, opt for a warm, welcoming smile that shows that you are happy to talk to them.

EXTRA **INFORMATION**

A simple "Good morning" or "Good after-noon" when the customer enters the shop, perhaps accompanied by "Can I help you?" is enough to open a dialogue and let the customer know that you are prepared to stop what you are doing to assist them.

2. Be welcoming

Non-verbal communication is vital. However nicely you speak, you will not make a good im-pression if you have your arms crossed (which suggests that you are withdrawn), shift your weight from one leg to the other (which suggests that you lack self-confidence) or keep your hands in your pockets (which suggest carelessness).

Your self-confidence and kindness should be clear not just in your words, but in your attitude. You need to work on your posture, facial expressions and behaviour in order to show their customer that they and their needs have your undivided attention. The following tips will help you:

- **smile** to show that you are welcoming and enthusiastic about the conversation;
- **stand up straight** to show that you are energetic and paying attention;
- **stay calm** to show that you are at ease and have a good knowledge of the subject at hand;
- **maintain eye contact** with the customer to show that you are direct and honest.

3. Adapt your approach to the customer

A good salesperson is like a chameleon: they can understand their customers and adapt to them. Their arguments should be based on the other person's knowledge (or lack thereof) of the product, range or brand. There is no point bombarding the customer with details and technical terms that they do not understand: they will simply be lost and feel that you are talking down to them.

Furthermore, you should adapt the way you talk to that of the potential customer (but make sure that you do not exaggerate and that you remain neutral and professional), as this will encourage them to identify with you and make them more likely to be won over by your arguments.

Something to avoid

There is nothing worse than a salesperson who makes clumsy attempts at humour. While it is permissible and even encouraged to joke a little with a customer once you have established a rapport, this does not mean scattering heavy-handed jokes throughout your sales pitch. The customer may end up not taking you seriously or thinking that you are making fun of them.

4. Never beg for the buyer's custom

Always keep in mind that a sale is a service for the customer and a way of responding to one of their needs. This means that the seller should never give the impression that they are asking for something from the prospect, because the customer needs the salesperson, their advice and their expertise just as much as the seller needs the consumer.

Nonetheless, make sure that you avoid coming across as pedantic or arrogant. A harmonious, effective salesperson-customer relationship is a balanced one in which each person respects the other and takes their needs into account.

WORK OUT WHAT THE CUSTOMER NEEDS

Not taking your prospect's needs into account is a surefire way to miss out on a sale. The customer's wishes are the backbone of the exchange: they guide it and give it purpose. All the strategies put in place by both the consumer and the seller aim to satisfy this need. You should therefore do everything you can to precisely identify exactly what the customer needs. This is the first challenge of business communication.

Understanding the customer's needs is essential to satisfying them. Although this point may seem obvious, in practice it is all too often ignored. Sellers cannot rely on their powers of persuasion alone: it is impossible to perfectly respond to the customer's needs without first identifying exactly what it is that they are looking for. This means that before you try to persuade, you need to try to understand.

This is a fundamental step of all sales strategies. The sales expert Michaël Aguilar explains that this "discovery phase" is essential for a successful conversation, and states that if sellers do not identify the customer's needs correctly or in enough detail, they are setting themselves up for objections and the refusal of their offer (2011: 80).

The SONCAS(E) model can be used to determine a prospect's needs. This system was developed by Bernard Julhiet (entrepreneur and specialist in business organisation and the training of sales forces) in the 1970s and is now widely known and used in France. It is used to distinguish between different categories of customers based on the most important criteria they use to make their choice. While products obviously respond to a range of criteria, all potential clients will attach varying degrees of importance to the different factors. The letters of the acronym stand for *Sécurité* ("Security"), *Orgueil* ("Pride"), *Nouveauté* ("Novelty/Technology"), *Confort* ("Comfort"), *Argent* ("Money"), *Sympathie* ("Sympathy") and

Écologie ("Ecology").

- **Security:** the customer is looking for a product that reassures them.
- **Pride:** they want to purchase something that makes them look good.
- **Novelty/Technology:** they want a recent product at the cutting edge of innovation.
- **Comfort:** the object needs to increase their wellbeing and make their life easier.
- **Money:** the customer wants the product to be cheap, or at least to have a good quality/price ratio.
- **Sympathy:** the person wants to feel comfortable with the seller and close the conversation with a purchase.
- **Ecology:** the product must respect the environment and be in accordance with sustainable development principles. The recent addition of this criterion has proved somewhat controversial, with some people arguing that it falls under pride, because the customer feels proud that they have done something good. Furthermore, it is worth asking whether or not environmental factors really influence the customer's choice.

5. Ask questions

The best – some would say the only – way to understand the customer and work out what they need is to ask them directly with relevant questions. To do this:

- **Work in stages.** Do not bombard the customer with a barrage of questions, but tailor your questions to their answers. There is no fixed plan to follow here; you will need to adapt your approach to the situation at hand.
- Get into the habit of asking **open questions**, meaning questions that call for a longer response rather than a simple "yes" or "no". You will get far more information out of a conversation by asking "What do you like about fantasy books?" than "Do you like this crime novelist?". This approach allows the customer to put their feelings into their own words. Even if the words they choose are somewhat vague, they will guide your investigation and will allow you to gradually home in on their needs.
- **Do not include the answer in the question.** The customer needs to feel free in their answer, and if you steer their response, you

may not be able to identify what they really need. For example, if you are talking to a customer looking for running shoes, ask them "How often do you go running?" rather than "How many times per week do you run?" In the latter case, an occasional jogger who goes for a run twice a month will be forced to either lie or skirt around the question, and may also feel guilty and think that they do not run enough.

SLOW AND STEADY WINS THE RACE

The seller who uses the farmer strategy (see "Over to you" section) can be illustrated perfectly by the story of the tortoise and the hare: rather than rushing to make a one-off sale, it is better to prepare effectively, take your time and really respond to the customer's needs in order to establish a sustainable relationship. Always remember that a happy customer is a loyal customer. Conversely, a person who feels that they have been tricked or taken advantage of not only is unlikely to come back, but may also badmouth you to their friends and family.

6. Reword the customer's comments

To make sure that you have fully grasped the customer's needs, get into the habit of rewording the information they tell you. Everyone talks differently, and all conversations can lead to misunderstandings, which is frustrating and a waste of time for both the customer and the seller. As you are the expert, your vocabulary will be more precise, and certainly different, from that of the customer. Their language may be vague, imprecise or even technically incorrect. Rewording is therefore a key technique to avoid getting the wrong idea.

The technique is simple: you need to combine the customers words with your own. This gives them the chance to confirm and possibly develop their comments, or to avoid misunderstandings by explaining what they really mean. This does not mean repeating what they say word for word, but expressing it differently, as illustrated below:

Sales techniques

	Without rewording	**Reworded**
Customer	Which of these two phones lasts the longest?	Which of these two phones lasts the longest?
Seller	Phone A lasts 36 hours and phone B lasts 48 hours.	In terms of battery life, phone A's is 36 hours and phone B's is 48 hours. However, in terms of overall product life, phone A is made by [brand], which is known for durability.

	Without rewording	**Reworded**
Customer	So that means that phone B is best?	I don't care that much about battery life, but I don't want to have to change my phone too often
Seller	If you're looking for a phone that will last a long time, it's better to go for that one.	In that case, I'd recommend phone A. We can also offer you an extended warranty, which means that you'll be able to keep your phone for longer.

In the first example, the seller misinterprets the customer's vague comments and recommends a product that will probably not suit their needs. Either the customer will buy the product and be unhappy with it, which means that they will not return to the shop, or the conversation will drag on for much longer before the seller understands the customer's needs, which will leave them both feeling impatient and frustrated. In this case, the customer risks leaving without buying anything.

Conversely, in the second example, the seller picks up on the double meaning in the customer's question and says it back to them. In this way, they provide more information while guiding the prospect towards the main criterion influencing their choice. This means that, in addition to recommending the most suitable product for the customer's needs, the seller can steer the conversation towards another product that they may be interested in (the extended warranty). The customer goes away satisfied and the sale has been successfully closed.

SOMETHING TO AVOID

Even if the customer asks a lot of questions, stay neutral and avoid giving your own opinion. Your role is to respond to a particular need, not to give your views on it.

FIND THE BEST SOLUTION

Once you have clearly identified the customer's needs, you can suggest the product(s) that will best respond to them. To ensure the best results, avoid rushing into things and adapt your arguments to your customer.

7. Keep it relevant

A good seller never describes all the product's capabilities. While it is important to have a good understanding of its features, you do not need to run through them exhaustively. Instead, you should develop your pitch based on what the customer says. This will give them the impression that you are paying attention to them as an individual and giving them good advice, which will make them more inclined to buy from you.

The customer's criteria as identified using the SONCAS(E) model can be very useful for selecting the arguments to highlight. For example, if your client does not care about novelty/technology, there is no point stressing the fact that a piece of furniture is exclusive to your shop and is made using a brand-new, cutting-edge material. You risk overwhelming them with information that they do not care about, losing their attention and reducing their motivation to make a purchase. If you have noticed that they care about the environment, it would be better to draw attention to the fact that the product was handmade by a local craftsman, so its carbon footprint is minimal.

8. Avoid criticising the competition

In all sectors, businesses face pressure from the competition. While competitiveness can help foster creativity and innovation, it is also one of the obstacles to closing a sale with a customer. This means that it is tempting to fall into the trap of putting your competitors down. However, in business as in life, criticising someone else is not the best way of selling yourself. Conversely, it suggests a degree of pettiness that reflects poorly on you, and reveals that your rivals are a real threat to your company.

When a prospect brings up your competitors, do not compare yourselves to them: instead, talk about your products and how they can respond to the customer's specific needs. Do not deny their weaknesses (because no product is perfect); instead, show that these weaknesses are far outweighed by their many advantages. Being honest with the customer will inspire trust and encourage them to make a purchase from you.

9. Do not put pressure on the customer

Hesitation is part and parcel of making a purchase. A customer with doubts is a thoughtful customer who wants to be sure that they are making the right decision. Consequently, if your pitch is clear and relevant and the product can fulfil the prospect's needs, there is an excellent chance that your conversation will end with a sale. The customer just needs a bit more time. Putting pressure on them is the last thing you should do.

If the person wants to end the conversation, there is no point in trying to cling to them by any means possible. Instead, you should be empathetic towards them: tell them that they can take as long as they need to think things over and that you are there to help if they have any further questions. In this way, the customer will feel listened to and understood from the beginning to the end of the conversation, which is rare in sales conversations.

EXTRA INFORMATION

Even if the customer does not come back to make the purchase you discussed with them, they will remember that you are a seller they can trust, that you are prepared to listen to them and that you give good advice. Far more than any sale, gaining the prospect's respect is the most difficult and most valuable achievement in the process, as this will ensure their loyalty.

10. Open the next conversation

Closing with an opening may seem contradictory, but it is the ultimate mark of a great seller. Whatever the outcome of the conversation, and whether or not you closed the sale, you should make the customer understand that the relationship of trust you have just built can continue in the future. There are many ways of leaving the door open: mentioning products related to the item in question, talking about the brand's upcoming releases or events, suggesting that the person tell you what they think of the product after they have used it, and letting them know that you remain at their disposal for any further advice or questions.

SUMMARY

The ten tips outlined in this chapter can be summarised in three points and a few key questions. These are the fundamental elements in any successful sale:

- **Pay attention to the customer.** Who are they? What do they want? What are they worried about? Your number one aim here is to make them feel comfortable, listen to them and be welcoming and empathetic towards them.

- **Identify their needs.** Does the customer have a precise idea of their needs? Does what they are asking for really correspond to their needs? The prospect should feel that the seller understands them and is capable of giving them good advice.
- **Suggest a solution.** Which product best responds to the need you have identified? Why? The seller needs to show that they understand which products are suited to their customer's needs, but also to let the customer choose and avoiding putting pressure on them.

TOP TIPS

Although no two sales situations are exactly the same and you will need to adapt your approach to your circumstances, the basic stages of the sales process can be summed up in a few key points. They form a guide which you can use as a starting point to develop your own sales style.

- **Greet the customer politely:** "Good morning/ good afternoon sir/madam."
- **Explicitly offer to help them:** "What can I do for you?", "Can I help you", "Are you looking for anything in particular?" If they say no, you can tell them "If you change your mind just ask, I'm here if you need any help."
- **Find out what the customer already knows:** "Are you already aware of our products/our brand?", "Why does this product interest you?"
- **Offer multiple solutions:** "It looks like a few of the products in our range could suit you", "There are a few things I can suggest."
- **Give your opinion:** "I think that this is the best match for what you're looking for", "I think

this solution would be best for you."

- **Take their opinion into account:** "What do you think?", "Does that seem OK to you?"
- **Offer more possibilities:** "Is there anything else that you need?", "Have you heard about our latest releases?", "Do you already have a loyalty card?", "Can I interest you in any additional options?"
- If you are busy with another customer, **let the next person know that you have seen them:** "Hello sir/madam, I'll be with you in just a moment", "I'll come to you next."
- **Mention the possibility of future contact:** "Feel free to come back later, I'm here if you need anything", "I'd love to know what you think of the product. If you want, you can come back and let me know", "I hope you like the product. Feel free to come back and let us know what you think of it."
- **End the conversation politely:** "Thank you, and see you again soon." Closing the sale is no reason to stop being polite.

While the wording you will use will vary based on the context and the other person (remember that you need to adapt your approach to the situation), the ten recommendations outlined above apply to virtually all successful sales and provide the framework for a productive business relationship. Each seller uses them in their own way so that they become an automatic part of their sales technique.

FAQS

HOW LONG SHOULD A SALE TAKE?

There is no fixed timeframe. Of course, an effective seller will close the sale quickly so that they can move on to the next prospect and boost their sales totals. However, ensuring customer satisfaction often takes time. You need to plan your arguments on a case-by-case basis: does the person have a precise idea of what they want? Are they in a rush? Do they ask a lot of questions? While the seller controls the pace of the conversation, it is the customer who determines how long it takes.

THE CUSTOMER HAS THEIR HEART SET ON A PARTICULAR PRODUCT, BUT I DO NOT THINK IT IS RIGHT FOR THEM. WHAT SHOULD I DO?

The seller's role is to give advice, but only the customer can make the final choice. You should therefore sincerely explain your opinion to them while accepting that they may disregard it.

Explain to the customer why, in your opinion, a particular product is better suited to their needs. If they are not open to your suggestion and remain set on their idea, there is no point digging your heels in; you risk wasting time and irritating the customer by questioning their judgement.

SHOULD I PROVIDE AN EXHAUSTIVE DESCRIPTION OF THE PRODUCT'S FEATURES?

No: all this will do is waste time and bore the customer. Even when a customer asks you for specific details on a product, they do not necessarily want to know everything. Not all information is interesting to all customers. It is up to the salesperson to figure out what they want (the SONCAS(E) model is useful for this) and adapt their arguments based on the customer's priorities.

Start by describing the product's general characteristics and adjust your pitch depending on the customer's reaction (or lack thereof): go into more detail about a feature that sparks their interest and pass over one that leaves them cold.

IS IT BETTER TO CONCEAL THE PRODUCT'S WEAK POINTS OR TO BE TRANSPARENT?

It goes without saying that successful sales are based on emphasising a product's strengths. However, this does not mean trying to disguise its weaknesses or lying to the customer. They will inevitably realise that they are being lied to and will then be unable to trust you. If a customer points out a weakness, explain to them that no product is completely perfect and that, while your product undeniably has its flaws, these are far outweighed by its many strong points that meet their needs.

A CUSTOMER IS TAKING UP A LOT OF MY TIME WHILE I HAVE OTHERS WAITING FOR ME. HOW CAN I CUT THE CONVERSATION SHORT WITHOUT LOSING THEM?

Some customers want to know absolutely everything about a particular product, while others struggle to make their mind up. In these cases, after answering all their questions and giving your opinion, give them some time to think things over. Tell them that you are going to give them a few minutes and come back so that they can tell you their decision. This will leave you free to talk to other customers and give them time to take your arguments on board.

THE CUSTOMER SEEMS TO BE WON OVER, BUT THEY WANT TO MAKE THE PURCHASE LATER. HOW CAN I CLOSE THE SALE NOW?

Sometimes, the prospect is not mentally ready to make a purchase. In this case, do not pressure them, but take the time to reassure them. To do this, the farmer strategy (see "Over to you" section) is often the most effective. Proceed methodically with the customer:

- **Understand what is stopping them from making a purchase.** Is the product not a perfect fit for them? Do they think it is too expensive? Do they need time to mentally prepare for the purchase? This analysis will allow you to select the strongest arguments.

- **Explain away their doubts.** What they want does not match up with what they really need; the product's price is in line with the market and its quality; once they have made the right choice (it is up to you to show them what this is), they will not regret their purchase.
- **Respond to their objections.** They will see that you are paying attention to them and will place their trust in you, which will encourage them to make the purchase.

THE CUSTOMER WANTS TO COMPARE MY OFFER WITH THE COMPETITION. HOW CAN I GET THEM TO BUY FROM ME?

While the seller should never be the one to bring up comparisons with the competition, they should be able to deal with this calmly under pressure from the customer.

In this case, try to show your products in the best possible light rather than criticising those of other companies. If you are left with no choice (because the customer explicitly brings it up), state the facts and stay objective. If your arguments are too subjective, the customer may go straight to the competition to get their opinion. If you focus on the facts, the customer will feel well-informed and free to make up their own mind. In addition to the objective reasons that you put forward so that they will make a purchase (the product's advantages), you will also create a subjective motivation (their trust in you) that they will not find with your competitors.

WHAT SHOULD I SAY TO THE CUSTOMER TO WIN THEIR LOYALTY?

There is no magic formula to generate customer loyalty. In general, if a customer is fully satisfied with their experience, they will want to come back. If they trust you, your judgement and your advice, they will not hesitate to buy from you again, and may even recommend you to their friends and family. Taking the time to listen to your customers and make them feel at home is therefore the best way of winning their loyalty.

OVER TO YOU

ARE YOU A HUNTER OR A FARMER?

We can distinguish two types of strategy for approaching the customer: the hunter and the farmer.

- **Hunters** skulk in the shadows and observe their prey so that they can target their action and act swiftly and precisely. They start by analysing the customer from a distance and interpreting their behaviour so that they can identify their profile as quickly as possible: what catches their eye? What do they linger over? Where to they tend to look for information? Before they even start talking to them, the hunter has an idea of their customer's profile and knows how to snare their prey.
For example, they will highlight the ergonomics and functionality of a camera to a customer who has been playing with multiple models, opening the lens, testing the zoom, and so on. Conversely, they will talk about the focal length and shutter speed to a customer

who has been browsing the technical information on each model.

- **Farmers** take their time and are calm and attentive. They approach the customer as soon as they come in, with no preconceptions about them, and adapt what they say as the conversation progresses. Like farming, building a relationship with the customer requires patience and attention. It is a process of familiarisation, and the seller's empathy builds trust with the customer. The salesperson helps the buyer to learn and shapes their opinion by providing them with the information they need.

  To work out what camera is best for the customer, the seller will try to get to know their personality and find out what kind of photographer they are: novice or expert; nomadic or sedentary; portrait, landscape, extreme sports or everyday scenes. They may also share their own experience.

To determine what kind of seller you are, answer "true" or "false" to the statements below.

- My motto is "time is money".
- A salesperson's effectiveness can be measured

by the number of buyers they can win over in
a day.
- Sales are like a sprint: the person who moves
the fastest gets to the finish line first.
- Drawing up a psychological profile of each
customer is a waste of time.
- Instincts are never wrong.

If you mainly answered "true", you are more of
a hunter. If you mainly answered "false", you are
more of a farmer.

BECOME A HUNTER-FARMER OR A FARMER-HUNTER

While the hunter is quick and effective and gets
straight to the point, the farmer leaves all their
options open. Hunters specialise in attracting
new customers, while farmers are good at crea-
ting customer loyalty, which in turn increases
sales. This means that the two types comple-
ment one another and are both indispensable to
a company's success.

A good salesperson knows whether they are a
hunter or a farmer; an excellent salesperson has
mastered both strategies and adapts their ap-

proach to each customer. To perfect your selling techniques, it is therefore important to learn the fundamental techniques of the opposite profile.

Tips to become a hunter or a farmer

To become a good hunter	To become a good farmer
• Ask as few questions as possible to identify what the customer needs. • Suggest the right product(s) quickly. • Briefly explain the relevant characteristics of the product.	• Take the time to get to know the customer and their personality. • Explore any possible related needs that they do not bring up unprompted. • Expand your arguments to cover several products

We want to hear from you!
Leave a comment on your online library
and share your favourite books on social media!

FURTHER READING

BIBLIOGRAPHY

- Aguilar, M. (2014) *Conclure la vente*. Paris: Éditions Dunod.

- Aguilar, M. (2011) *Vendeur d'élite. Les techniques et secrets dévoilés des meilleurs vendeurs*. Paris: Éditions Dunod.

- Chabry, L., Gillet-Goinard, F. and Jourdan, R. (2014) *La boîte à outils de la relation client*. Paris: Éditions Dunod.

- Tzu, S. (2017) *The Art of War*. Seattle: AmazonClassics.

ADDITIONAL SOURCES

- Adamson, B. and Dixon, M. (2013) *The Challenger Sale: How to Take Control of the Customer Conversation*. London: Penguin.

- Blount, J. (2017) *Sales EQ: How Ultra-High Performers Leverage Sales-Specific Emotional Intelligence to Close the Complex Deal*. Hoboken, New Jersey: John Wiley & Sons, Ltd.

- Kensett, H. (2016) *Sales Mind: 48 tools to help you*

sell. London: Profile Books Ltd.

- Peiffer, C. (2016) *The Art of Convincing*. Trans. Lunt, E. Brussels: Plurilingua Publishing.

- Swinscoe, A. (2016) *How to Wow: 68 Effortless Ways to Make Every Customer Experience Amazing*. Harlow: Pearson Education Limited.

IMPROVE YOUR GENERAL KNOWLEDGE

IN A BLINK OF AN EYE !

www.50minutes.com